THE SHOWMEN'S FORGOTTEN SCAMMELLS

By Kay Townsend

Front cover illustrations by Louise Mowlem

PETER BENNETT
01329 846898

Published in 2007

© Kay Townsend
Email: kay58@fsmail.net

ISBN 13: 978-0-9553595-1-4

Also written by Kay Townsend:

Townsends – A Showman's Story

Cover design and print by

Creeds the Printers, Broadoak, Bridport, Dorset DT6 5NL

I hope you enjoy this book, as much as I have writing it.

Email: kay58@fsmail.net

Telephone: (01305) 778693

Kay Townsend

ACKNOWLEDGEMENTS

I would like to thank the following people for their help in compiling this book.

My husband, David Castleman
My daughter, Joe Castleman
Mr Barry Brown
Mr Stephen Smith

Mr D. Gillard
Mr Jim Wells
Mr Terry Norman
Mr D. Hallett

Scammell 1: *'Vanguard'*
Mr P. Townsend, Mr M. Herbert and Mr D. Cave

Scammell 2: *'Empress of England'*
Mr C. Evans and Mr C. Hill

Scammell 3: *'Rocket'*
Mr C. Heal, Mr J. Clements and Mr D. Langley

Scammell 4: *'Earl Kitchener'*
Mr H. Studt

Scammell 5: *'John Bull'*
Mr P. Studt

Scammell 6: *'Earl Bettie'*
Mr E. De Vey, Mr G. De Vey and Mr G. Lewis

Scammell 7: *'Dreadnought'*
Mr M. Stabb and Mr B. Whitelegg

Scammell 8: *'Impregnable'*
Mr M. Stabb

Scammell 9: *'Mascot'*
Mr T. Harniess, Mr R. Eddy, Mr P. Procter, Brian & Ben Freer and the late Mr G. Procter

Scammell 10: *'No 1'*
Mr T. Harniess, Mr D. Vickers and Mr J. Schofield

I would also like to thank the friends that have helped with information and supplied photos for this book.

Every care has been taken that the material in this book does not infringe copyrights. I would like to apologise if material in this publication offends anyone. Unaccredited photos belong to the Kay Townsend collection.

DEDICATION

I would like to dedicate this book to my cousin
Paddy Townsend.

This is my second book to include details of
my family's transport.

Paddy and I have spent many hours talking of
how it was years ago on the road.

Without his wonderful stories my work would not have been the same.

CONTENTS

INTRODUCTION
How they came to be 1
Before you start to read about... 4

THE SCAMMELLS

Scammell 1	R. Townsend	'Vanguard' BJT 726	11
Scammell 2	B. Hill	(No name) DVJ 45	25
Scammell 3	A. Heal	'Rocket' JHU 632	35
Scammell 4	A. L. Studt	'Earl Kitchener' JC 8358	43
Scammell 5	J. P. Studt	'John Bull' EYC 38	47
Scammell 6	Anderton & Rowland	'Earl Beatty' CJY 965	51
Scammell 7	T. Whitelegg	'Dreadnought' GFJ 331	59
Scammell 8	T. Whitelegg	'Impregnable' GFJ 330	65
Scammell 9	F. Harniess	'Mascot' DDT 32	69
Scammell 10	T. Harniess	'No. 1' DDT 107	85

HOW THEY CAME TO BE

In 1946 the Scammell works at Watford had 10 surplus 45-ton chain drive Scammells for sale. There were about 50 made of this model, some you would have recognised as going to Pickfords for haulage. Two were sold during the war for timber work to Fisher Renwick, but 10 were held back just in case the M.O.D. required them for war work, which they did not, so when the war was over, they were going cheap as Watford wanted to clear them out to make way for the new model, the Showtrac.

The agent to the showmen, on behalf of Scammell, was Sydney Harrison of Bury St Edmonds. I discovered years ago that anything going cheap, the showman would give it a go and snap up the bargains.

The chain drive was seen as a bargain at the time, at the starting price of only £1945. Each showman's price of his Scammell would vary, depending on what he ordered with his lorry. For example, spare 40 by 8" tyre & rim £24, Ballast box body £34, power take off fitted to gear box £60. Also stated on invoice 'Cover for Sidney Harrison £182'. I think this would have been his commission for the sale. The showmen could pay a little extra and have the optional winch and dynamo. The winch was an extra £225, however there was a 12.5% discount for some reason, so they only paid £196.17 shillings and 6 pence. The price of the dynamo on the back, to power the rides, was not included on information sheets from Leyland.

A basic invoice sheet reads as follows:

> **Invoice No L4431**
>
> SCAMMELL HEAVY DUTY CHAIN DRIVE TRACTOR CHASSIS mounted on 40 by 8" tyres, singles on front wheels, twins on driving wheels. Chassis fitted with Gardner 6LW. Diesel engine, 4 speed gearbox, heavy duty bevel driven counter shaft with chain drive to road wheels. Chassis complete with front and rear wings. Toolkit and 12 ton hydraulic jack.
>
> C.A.V. 12 volt lighting and starting set. Comprising of dynamo, battery starter, two head, two side and one tail lamps.
>
> SALOON TYPE DRIVERS CAB with opening windscreen and bench type seats.
>
> NEATES TRAILER BRAKES fitted.
>
> BRAKE AIR RESERVOIR To be in standard position on top of frame behind cab.
>
> EXHAUST PIPE to run up back of cab.
>
> REAR TOWING ATTACHMENT with drawbar guides to be fitted.
>
> CHROME WHEEL CAPS Two coats of works grey.
>
> GUARANTEE standard six Months.

I would like to thank the BRITISH COMMERCIAL VEHICLE MUSEUM, LEYLAND for their help with some details within this book.

CUSTOMER   Sidney Harrison Ltd.,

TYPE   45-ton Tractors.

<u>MR. BLADES</u>.

    Please note that the standard 12 & 19 tooth sprocket adaptor sets as called for on the Index are to be supplied and fitted to each of the tractors.

    If it is not possible to fit winches to these Tractors prior to delivery they are to be modified as far as possible to accommodate winches at a later date with the minimum of difficulty.

                                  SALES DEPARTMENT.

BEFORE YOU START TO READ ABOUT...

...the 45 ton chain drive, I would like you to read the following information, so that you may understand more about the model.

I would first like you to read a letter from Scammell of Watford, to a Mr Gerry Procter, regarding some questions he had when he first purchased his Scammell from Mr Gordon Eddy.

Scammell Lorries Ltd
WATFORD HERTS ENGLAND

Telephone:

DAT Line
Watford 44211 (P8X

Our ref, KI/PH/T.PUBS. 19118

Night Line after 5.30pm
Watford 43731

14th March 1967
Mr G. W. Proctor,
Copmanthorpe, York.

Dear Sir,

Further to your letter of the 8th instant re 1946 Scammell Tractor chassis No. 1959, we will answer your letter in the order of your queries.

1. The vehicle was designed to operate air pressure brakes on the trailer only and this was operated by means of the hand brake lever. Two hand levers were fitted, one operating the trailer brakes, the other operated internal expanding brakes on the rear axle. The foot brake

operated the transmission brake and it was never recommended that the foot brake should be used for long periods, due to the possibility of over heating the drum. Assuming that the brake gear was returned to its original concept it would definitely not meet with the present impending M.O.T. braking regulation, as you will appreciate there are no brakes on the front axle.

2. The vehicle was rated as a 45 ton tractor, this of course will be in low gear.

3. The original tyre equipment was 36 by 8 front & 13.5 by 20 LP rear.

4.
Front axle swivel pins:	fill caps with engine oil
Steering box:	Shell Spirax
Engine:	Rotalla 20/20w
Air Compressor:	Engine oil
Geart Box	Equal quantities of Shell Triple and Shell Spirax
Jack Shaft	Equal quantities Shell Triple and Shell Spirax

Yours faithfully,

SCAMMELL LORRIES LIMITED.

K. J. MARTIN,
TECHNICAL PUBLICATIONS

The Transmission Brake

As the brake is situated in the centre of the chassis on the propshaft, grease would gct on the plate/drum, from a nearby seal and the nearby greased chains.

If the chains were a little over greased, they would flap and splatter grease everywhere, also Scammell did warn that the drum was prone to over-heating. When the brake was applied and the pads clamped the drum, this caused the brake to smoke, which consequently filled the cab with smoke and fumes.

Throttle and Chains

One advantage this model had, if a showman now changing from steam power over to diesel and did not have a generator, he could drive the Scammell on to blocks to level the lorry, then he could remove the chains from the driveshaft sprocket, and a thinner chain was led from the sprocket to a dynamo upon the back of the lorry. A hand throttle near the steering column could then be used to control the speed of the engine, thus driving the dynamo, which supplied the power for the rides. Only one family in this book, Whitelegg's, used V belts instead of chains.

Hand Throttle on steering column.

Small bolt linking the chain.

The chains were removed and reattached by a nut and bolt, forming the link. A split pin was also put through the bolt to secure it. One man could do this job, however, he needed two pairs of hands, so string was threaded through the chain, then pulled, which drew the chain ends together.

*An excellent view before the chains are removed,
the sprocket being 9½ inches across. Chain width being 3⅜ inch.*
From the Ben Freer collection.

*Chain drive DDT 107, first registered 1946 at Doncaster.
Ready to supply the extra power.*
*From the British Vehicle Museum, Leyland.
Taken by Scammell Lorries Ltd.*

Sprocket on dynamo shaft, chains would lead from this to the drive shaft below.

The Jack / driveshaft with the chains removed.
From the Colin Evans collection.

The information you are about to read in this book has come from the owner / drivers of these Scammells, who have seen and checked the manuscripts before print.

Therefore, all details are cleared by them. This book is not recycled information from other publications.

SCAMMELL 1

'Vanguard' BJT 726

Photo courtesy of Mr Richard Collis. Taken in 1972.

In 1946, the West Country showman Richard Townsend decided to order a Scammell and phase out the traction engine, so my family bought one of the 45 ton chain drive Scammells from Watford through the agent Sidney Harrison and named her *'Vanguard'*.

The late Richard Townsend.

11

She was bought on the 15 April 1946, and was chassis number 1958. Before a member of the family could leave the factory with her, they first had to drive on a practice pad, to show they were able to handle her on the road.

My uncle, Marshall Herbert, had only been used to driving a traction engine up until now, and he was the first member of the family to drive our new Scammell. He collected her from the Scammell works at Watford, and drove to the Fairfield's car park at Dorchester, Dorset, where my family were open at the time.

He said at the time that it was such a bad experience he vowed never to drive her again. Speed could not have been the factor here, as her top speed was 20 mph and that was down hill, the average being 15mph.

When the family paid for her, they travelled by train to collect her carrying suitcases full of half crowns and two shilling pieces as well, but at £1945 a large percentage would have been notes as well and that's how they paid for her.

She was basic, so did not come with the optional dynamo or winch.

1946. Feeling proud with the new Scammell, with no body on her yet.
Taken by cousin, Denny Cave, at Bakers Ground, Portland, Dorset.

In all honesty, they were not a good buy, as the chain drive was slow and messy. However you will read later how the chain drive proved its capability and strength.

Just like the other Scammells, she was just a chassis cab when new so we had to add the body to her, which my family built themselves. Just like the others when new, she was plain grey in colour, and came with her own toolbox that consisted of a spanner, which fitted everything.

At first, there was a lot of trouble with her fuel, only to discover that the fuel tank had rust in it. We contacted Watford to tell them. The reason they gave was that they made so many fuel tanks; they were stood around for a while before being fitted. They did not supply a new one, instead we managed to clean ours out.

Another problem they had, was the manual that came with her stated that they had to turn a brass cap, which was full of grease, the turning would spread grease on the clutch shaft. The family did not realise this had to be done. One day Dick Townsend was driving her, and the clutch seized up. When he pushed the clutch down, it went straight to the floor, (fast). Men came a considerable distance to repair the clutch, but we are not sure where from.

Being chain-driven there were two chains, one either side leading from the drive shaft to the back axle.

Picture by Mr C Evans.

Above, you will notice the teeth around the brake drum. When the drum is in place, the chain leads around this to the sprocket on the drive/Jack shaft (on the left of picture).

Rear view.

This picture is of a Scammell with a 19 teeth sprocket, so by law she could tow 45 tons, 3 trailers, or up to 90 feet.

However, by changing to a <u>smaller</u> sprocket, and adding 6 more links to the chain she would be much slower, 5-10 mph but the tow weight was higher. The smaller sprocket is situated behind the 19 teeth, so all you need to do is remove the 19 teeth and your smaller one is already in place.

30 Teeth.

By changing the size of the sprocket, to a larger one, (30 teeth), they would drive faster, up to 30 mph, but the tow weight would be reduced.

These Scammells came with the same engine, a Diesel 6 LW Gardner doing about 10 miles to the gallon.

The Townsend family still had one traction engine, '*Queen Mary*' on the road, so for two years, both traction engine and Scammell worked alongside one another and with the Scammell being slow, they worked well together. In 1946 the family were buying something called gas oil for the Scammell, which was really diesel but with no tax, so it was cheaper to buy at only one shilling per gallon. Then the Government wanted more tax, so red dye was added to some diesel, but lorries had to be run on white diesel now, and the cost went up to half a crown a gallon.

They had to keep the traction engine travelling as well because it was not until 1947, one year after they bought the Scammell, that they finally put the body and dynamo on the back, so for one year she remained a chassis cab and just towed on the road. The '*Queen Mary*' was retired in 1948.

Supplying the power at night

When ordering her new, the request was no cast iron ballast block, therefore before we could have the body fitted on the back of her in 1947, a concrete ballast was put down in the floor to add weight to her and also to attach steel runners on to which then a dynamo was bolted to the runners. The only thing we put in the back of the body was a Phoenix 500 amps dynamo. They drove the Scammell to Bath to collect it. The dynamo drove the Ark ride and lights when open.

The Ark, she had to power and tow on the road.

This meant every new place visited, the Scammell was driven on blocks to level her. Then as she was a chain drive, her two road chains were removed and two thinner chains were led up from the driveshaft/Jackshaft up through the floor inside the body to two 7 inch sprockets, one on each side of the dynamo.

Then she would be put in 4th gear, using the additional hand throttle, which would keep her running continually at approx 1000 revs, driving the dynamo in the back of her at 500 revs. This hand throttle was no good for driving on the road as she would only end up travelling at 10 mph, but it was ideal for driving the dynamos for the showman.

The Scammell had many drawbacks – here are just a few...

When in a muddy field, she would always get stuck. She did not like soft ground at all, and had to be winched out many times.

Also, she was uncomfortable as the seats were just wood with a thin layer of horse hair covered by leather. As my Uncle Dick was short, his legs were not long enough to reach the pedals, so they put blocks on the pedals to make them higher up.

She had four gears, plus reverse. When changing from 3rd to 4th, as long as you remembered to double de-clutch, you were OK. She was very low geared; so much so you could pull away in top. However, she had to almost stop in order to change into bottom gear before pulling a steep hill.

There is one particular hill in Somerset, called Wynyard's Gap, which is known to be very long and steep, and towing two trucks it would take about 30 mins for her to pull it.

Another problem this model had was that the peddles were hard to push down. Paddy Townsend would push down the accelerator, then place his other leg on top of that one by crossing his ankles, the weight of both legs on the peddle made it a little easier.

Another problem was that the chains had to be greased, then when the chains turned they would splatter grease all over. In our case because we had a full box body on her, so the body was splattered with grease inside.

On the road, the noise inside the body from the chains was deafening, as the chains rattled within the chain guards.

The block boy riding on the open truck behind

For the first few years there was a young man called Ralph Castleman who would ride on the open truck that was being towed behind. His job was to take care of the brakes on the two trucks when they were either about to climb a hill or go down one.

As it was law then, that you had to have one person riding with the load for each truck you tow, sometimes there were 2 block boys.

Pulled over here for lunch, taken 17/4/55,
coming out of Beaminster (Dorset).
Courtesy of the Stuart Beaton collection.

When approaching the top of a hill, before she could go down it, one toot on the horn would tell the block boy to jump off the truck behind, while they were still moving (about 3 mph). The boys would run down one side of the load and apply the brake handles on both trucks, then the Scammell would be put into bottom/ crawler gear.

The brakes on the trucks would be left on down over the hill in order to hold back the two trucks. This would help prevent the weight from pushing the Scammell forward, as the two trucks' combined weight was more than the Scammell, the Scammell being about 9 ton.

When they were on level road again, two toots on the horn would then tell the block boy to let both the brake handles off again on both trucks. When the boy had done this, he would then run <u>between</u> the back of the lorry and truck (still moving), climb up on the high draw/tow bar, and sit back on the truck being towed. (Can you imagine what health and safety would say nowadays?)

By the time they had reached the bottom of the hill, the brakes on the truck were very hot, and smelling so too.

As she was only a small Scammell there was the risk of her being pulled backwards when going <u>up</u> hills.

Therefore, they had to make sure she was in bottom gear <u>before</u> starting to pull. They could not risk slowing to a stop, in order to change gear, once they were so far <u>up</u> as she could have been pulled backwards by the combined weight of the two trucks.

However, the block boy always knew there were blocks on the truck to quickly put behind the wheels if anything like this should happen.

After a few years the block boy was no longer needed, as the drivers got to know the lorry/gear box well, and how steep the hills were around here. Besides, there was always a chap in the passenger seat to jump out if need be.

The addition of air brakes were fitted in later years.

When we want to stop

Years ago it was <u>legal</u> for persons to ride up in the living wagons whilst on the road, however, with travel being so slow, sometimes whoever was in the wagon needed to stop for a while. So this is what Townsends did. A piece of string was led from the living wagon, along the load into the Scammell cab, to which the string was tied to a bell. If they needed to stop, in the wagon, all they did was pull the string and ring the bell.

Scrumping with a Scammell

When Paddy Townsend was young, he would be block boy sometimes, riding on the swinging boat truck being towed. As the Scammell was so slow, she was ideal for apple scrumping. The Scammell never stopped throughout the following sequence I am about to explain to you.

There was a particular orchard in Somerset where Paddy would jump off the truck and into the orchard with his sack bags, whilst the Scammell carried on.

He quickly filled his sacks with apples, listening all the time for the Mack lorry which was on its way. Cousin Bernard would be the last to leave the field, driving the Mack. He would easily catch up. He would stop at the orchard to collect Paddy, who would climb in the Mack cab with his bags of apples. Bernard would then drive as fast as he could to catch up with the Scammell. When he did, Paddy would jump out, run and jump upon the swinging boat truck again.

The timing was crucial, as near Crewkerne (Somerset), there is a steep hill and the Scammell would need her block boy. They never got their timing wrong. Also Paddy's dad, who drove the Scammell, never let on if he knew he was without a block boy for a few miles.

Scammell and the ducks

When we attended a charter street fair in the village of Wool, Dorset, all space was taken up because the street was small so the Scammell was parked across the stream, which ran along one side of the street. Whoever had to drop her chains for opening, would have to put their wellington boots on and get in the stream to do so, being careful not to get a wet behind. Of course all lorries, especially with greasy chains, would leak a little oil. Although it not being much, it leaked into the stream.

A little further down stream a gentleman kept ducks. One day he asked us, quite nicely, if we could not put our Scammell over the stream, as his ducks were getting oil around their bodies. We of course obliged, and moved the Scammell.

They have worked harder than any man, but when they made them that was the plan

One summer the Mack lorry, with the 2 Ark trucks behind, broke down on Weymouth esplanade, causing havoc with the traffic. The police just wanted it moved. It was decided to let the Scammell tow the complete load as it stood.

With a police escort, she towed through the town, then there is a 1 in 9 hill called Boot Hill, which is on the edge of the town. Paddy Townsend was driving her at the time and making sure she was in bottom gear, slowly and with some difficulty, she only just pulled the hill as her engine loudly barked.

The load she had to tow. Photo by the late Allen Imber.

They were on their way to Portland at the time. When Paddy arrived, the rest of the men came over and said they could not believe he had taken such a chance, as they did not think she could do it.

In order to test the lorries out at Watford, before any Scammell left the factory, they first were made to pull a 1 in 5 hill, towing their full load. So that day when *'Vanguard'* pulled the 1 in 9 Boot Hill, she proved without a doubt her capability.

Leaving Sherborne, heading for Mere Carnival 3/9/1972.
From the Alan Imber collection.

At the end of the 1972 season, the Scammell went into retirement and remained under the sheds in the yard covered over for a few years, until one of our other lorries let us down one year. Then the Scammell came out of retirement for one summer only, then she was returned to the sheds again.

In 1989, there was some cosmetic work done on her by a Mr Tye of Weymouth.

Courtesy of M P I Services of Weymouth.

Also in 1989, Tom Townsend decided to sell the two rides, the Dodgems and Ark and also the Scammell, which he sold to a dealer. Then she seemed to disappear. Remember the Scammell had been with us for 43 years and we, the 4th generation, had grown up with her always being there, so we wondered what had happened to her?

The family spread word that we were trying to trace the Scammell, and for 13 years she just went astray. Then in 2001, the family finally found her again.

SCAMMELL 2

Bernard Hill's DVJ 45

Photo by permission of Mr C. Evans.

Bernard Hill was a friend of my grandfather, and these two friends each had one of the 45 ton CDs from Watford.

DVJ 45, chassis number 1962, was registered to Showman Bernard Hill on the 3rd June 1946, at Hereford, then later Park Street, Bristol. She travelled around the West Country Fairs, as well as the Midlands, Shropshire, Hereford and Wales.

Seen here during her working life. Taken at Horfield Bristol. *The late Bernard Hill in 1960.*

Copyright of Surrey History Centre.

Bernard Hill decided <u>not</u> to have the optional winch, but did pay the extra and have the dynamo; however this was used very little.

She would have to do the journey to the new place of opening twice or sometimes three times. First, she would tow the Dodgems, and then have to return to do a second trip taking the living wagon.

The family would open every Saturday during the winter months at Kidderminster. In order to save money they would only tax the Scammell, but the Mack lorry had to go as well as it had the generators on the back. Therefore, the Scammell would tow the Mack.

From the Barry Brown collection.

Below, a trouble-some transmission brake.

Because when the brakes were applied and the pad clamped the drum, causing the cab to fill with smoke and fumes, Bernard Hill uncoupled his foot brake.

A man called Cecil Mutton, known as 'Crips', would usually drive the Bernard Hill Scammell on the road. In fact 'Crips' was so used to driving her, that sometimes he would really let her go down hills. However on one occasion going down Pen Mill Hill, between Sherborne and Yeovil, he was approaching some road works, the sign was on STOP but 'Crips' could not stop due to the fact that the foot brake had been uncoupled, and it was only the hand brake.

So he had to decide, did he veer left and drive over the hole in the road (which had workmen in), or did he take the chance and go through the STOP sign and hope for the best? The workman holding the STOP sign could see this lorry careering towards him at some speed, so at the last minute he changed the sign to GO, much to 'Crips' relief.

But afterwards everyone had a laugh, because if he had decided to veer left and drive over the hole in the road, what would have been the reaction of the workmen, seeing the chassis of a chain drive and two trucks passing over the top of them?

Also when the Scammell picked up too much speed towing the two Dodgem trucks, 'Crips' sometimes would steer so that the front of the truck being towed would touch the grass bank/verge, to slow the load down a little.

His brother 'Lego Mutton' would also drive the Scammell.

Again on one occasion, whilst going down a steep hill with the 2-dodgem trucks, the Scammell picked up too much speed. 'Lego' shouted to the chap riding with him "Open the bloody door and get ready to jump, I can't hold her back!"

'Lego' spotted a field where the gate had been left open, so he steered her into the field. Because the weight of the two trucks was pushing her forward, she entered the field at some speed. However, as the tyres left the tarmac and hit the grass, she gradually slowed down. 'Lego' drove the load around the field and straight back out of the gate.

A member of the family, Clifton Hill, told me that sometimes the driver's leg would get tired on the accelerator as the pedals were so hard to press down. When Clifton was young he would hold the pedal down for the drivers until his leg also got tired. He could do this because there is room for a small person to sit between the driver and the driver's door. The steering wheels are not central in these Scammells, however, they are slightly away from the door.

Up until 1967, 3 years after Bernard Hill died, the Scammell was still being used.

When finally sold she fell into the hands of a Mr Jesse Vines, who did not register her despite owning her for about 4 years. Then he sold her to Mr Colin Evans who bought the lorry from Mr Vines in about 1972.

Now in preservation

In February 2006, at a rally meet at Gillingham, Dorset, I came across the Bernard Hill Scammell. The owner Mr Colin Evans gave some details of how he came to own her. In 1972, he found a Mr Jesse Vines at Gloucester had two chain drives which had been stood along side each other. Mr Evans, when looking, had the choice of the two, both were the same price £300 each, it was a matter of take your pick. However, Mr Evans at the time was not keen on paying £300, so he decided to leave it.

He returned several times and it was obvious the man was not coming down in price, so he went for the ex-Bernard Hill one DVJ 45, which incidentally, out of the two, needed more work doing to it.

When he went to collect her, he could not start her due to the lack of compression. So they gave the Scammell a tow to start her and drove her on to the low loader. However, Colin knew that when he got her home he would have the same problem and would not be able to start her to drive her <u>off</u> the low loader so they <u>left her engine running</u> all the way to her new home in Bristol.

On arrival they unloaded her down the lane and then drove her into the yard, much to the dismay of Colin's father who was wondering what on earth he had brought home this time!

The dynamo, which had been in the back of her and used by Bernard Hill, had been removed and is now on the showman's traction engine *'Sir John Fowler'*. The Hills' name plate is still on the dynamo to this day.

Colin Evans had to recondition her engine as it needed doing when he bought her from Mr Vines, then one winter he forgot to drain the water from the engine and the frost cracked the head, the engine had to be stripped down again.

The first time Colin Evans drove her, he had to take her down a hill at Shepton Mallet (Somerset). He was not aware of the reputation of the foot brakes on these as no one had told him. When going down the hill at Shepton Mallet, he naturally used the foot brake and could not figure out what was wrong when his cab filled with smoke. He pulled over to look under the lorry, and found the brake looking slightly red, so he had to wait for it to cool.

Colin Evans bought her to tow a trailer with his Bryan Donkin steam stationary engines on, visiting various rallies.

From the Colin Evans collection.

However, people were starting to show interest in the Scammell as well.

He would regularly take part in road runs with the Scammell and would join half way through the run, due to her top speed only being 15 mph.

Whilst in the ownership of Bernard Hill she was not named, but now she is.

'Empress of England'

At the Stourpaine Bushes Steam Fair in the 1980s, 3 Scammell shaft drives coupled together got stuck and failed to pull a large tree on a timber carriage.

(Now you must try to picture what I am describing to you of what happened).

The following night, 3 of the 45 ton CD's attempted the same pull. Led by Colin's Scammell, a straight bar coupled to another chain drive, the ex Whitelegg (Impregnable), then another straight bar coupled to Derek Hallett's ex timber chain drive which was coupled to the timber carriage loaded with trees.

So there were three 45-ton chain drives with a timber carriage. The lead Scammell, Colin with the ex Bernard Hill attempted to pull the lot. Half way through the lorry pull, Colin said he did not think his Scammell would make it, but she did, and boy did she smoke!

The only photo we know of taken at the time.
Photo from the Colin Evans collection.

When it was all over, people came over to the arena and shook his hand and said that they had never seen anything like it before. The men decided not to let one chain drive pull the lot again, as Colin knew the strain did not do her engine any good.

Due to his workload in 1980, Colin Evans stopped doing the rallies, so the ex Bernard Hill Scammell was parked up and covered over for over 20 years.

It is strange that he just bought the Scammell to tow his engines about, but during the 20 year stop-gap, people were asking where the Scammell was.

In 2003, he unwrapped and started to restore her again which took two years.

Photos from the Collin Evans collection.

Colin Evans has restored her twice. In the 2003 restoration the wood frame of the body needed replacing, but the alloy panels were OK so he made a new frame and just put back the original panel. She can now be seen regularly around West Country rallies.

'Gentle Giant' courtesy of Derek Hallett.

Derek Hallett's 45-ton chain drive FTD 812, chassis No 1897, is the other chain drive which took part in the lorry pull at the steam fair. (In the ex Bernard Hill story.)

Although she does not have a showman's pedigree, she is the same model.

At the beginning I mentioned 2 were released earlier than the others from Watford (during 1943) for timberwork, this was one of them. The company that bought them were Fisher Renwick.

With the 10 that went to showmen and the 2 bought for timber work, I have accounted for 12 of the 50 made. Remember earlier in this chapter, when Colin Evans went to buy his Scammell, and it was parked next to another one? Well this was the one. But not looking as good as she does today.

This is the brass plate from the Hallett Scammell with her details on. All the Scammells would have had one of these in the cab. However, very few exist, because over the years they have been removed as keepsakes.

SCAMMELL 3

'Rocket' JHU 632

Taken in Midsomer Norton, 1967.
From the David Langley collection.

'Rocket' chassis no 1961, was bought on 28th May 1946, by the showman Albert Heal of Bristol. The Heal family paid a little extra for their model, as it came with the optional winch and a Mawdsley 400 amp dynamo.

Both the originals are still on her to this day.

ALTERATION TO SALES ORDER
SALES ORDER NO: 8310

CUSTOMER: Sidney Harrison,
TYPE: 45 ton Tractor.

Mr Blades

Please note that two 46 teeth dynamo sprockets, Part No 37/94 are to be supplied in connection with the above tractor when supplies become available.

From the note from Sidney Harrison to Scammell, it looks like they run out of sprockets when it came to the Albert Heal order.

As she was supplied as a chassis cab when new, Albert took the Scammell to coach builders at Downend for the body to be built.

She travelled around 6 counties, Devon, Somerset, Wiltshire, Avon Gloucestershire and London, towing and supplying the power to the family ride The Moon Rocket, hence the Scammell got its name.

1939, by Alan Southwood.

The Rocket ride was not only a heavy ride to travel with, taking up to 9 hours to build up, but also it was a heavy ride to power.

When the ride was turned on, you could hear the 6.L Gardner engine working hard as the governors opened to provide the extra power as the ride pulled away.

In about 1964, the Heal family sold the Moon Rocket ride, so her job now, like the other chain drive Scammells, was to tow and power the Dodgems.

Photo by Mr Jim Wells.

You will notice that the fuel tank is within the body on this one. I have not seen this on any of the others. At one time she suffered with air lock problems, so the tank was placed higher, by putting it in the body for gravity feed. This is the original fuel tank, as the step for getting up into the cab, can still be seen on the tank.

On the road now she would tow 2 Dodgem trucks and Albert's living wagon.

Due to the law at the time, Albert had 2 and sometimes 3, block / brake boys, one sat on each Dodgem truck and one sat up in the living wagon.

I have mentioned before how hard it was to press down the pedals on this model. Well, on one occasion, Charles Heal who would drive her sometimes, remembers how one day he did so many miles, that his feet were red raw by the end of the day.

Almost a runaway

In later years Charles Heal was driving the Scammell from Weston Super Mare, to Seaton. Just outside Chard, there is a hill that he did not realize was so steep; he automatically slammed her in low gear. He was pulling 3 trucks at the time and he could feel her speed getting out of hand, so he had 3 men with him pulling on the brake of each truck, while he pulled the hand-brake on the Scammell, which was air brake; also by using the foot brake as well, he stopped the runaway.

Charles said it was frightening at the time, so much so, he left her in bottom gear for the next 3 miles!

She was retired in 1972 and was stored at the family yard at Bedminster, nr Bristol, and unseen for 8 years.

During 1979/80 she was restored for Albert Heal, by John Clements and Raymond Bryant. The work took 6 weeks.

She was taken down to the steel plate, and then they lined it with alloy. The body was rebuilt the same shape as the original, even the trap door in the roof of the body is there, which I presume is for lifting the dynamo out through the top. The roller shutters are the originals.

When the cab was rebuilt, they also needed to replace the headlights and were lucky to find two on a shelf in a shop that were really for an old car, but were suitable for the Scammell. The new leather top for the seat was made by another showman, Maureen Appleton.

The engine needed another starter and dynamo, but apart from that it was OK.

The first time starting her with the rope on the starting handle, took 3 pulls before she fired up, then the engine was missing badly for about 10 minutes, then she finally cleared, and was running smoothly.

Also at the restoration, her name was changed to *'Prince Albert'*.

Albert Heal (centre), with John Clements and Raymond Bryant, who did her restoration work. Photo courtesy of John Fleming.

When she was finished they drove her to Albert's house for him to see, and he could not believe how good she looked.

Next, she attended their 50th wedding anniversary party, at which she supplied the power to a fair ground organ.

'Prince Albert' returns to the road.
From the Geoff Slade collection.

The picture above was taken with her out travelling again, as after the restoration, she returned to the road with Jimmy Smart for a short time. She was still working with the Heal's Dodgems and Big Wheel.

She has everyone's attention here at Taunton, as her winch pulls out the E R F.
Photo courtesy of Geoff Slade.

Her winch was also now being used to winch up the towers, when building up the Big Wheel.

*Having trouble here coming out of Taunton,
notice the truck belly box has hit the grass bank.*
Photo by Geoff Slade.

All 10 of these Scammells worked hard for long hours, the showmen definitely got their money's worth from them, but when talking about this one, I somehow feel *'Rocket'* worked harder then the others. Travelling 6 counties, always towing 3 loads behind her, including Albert's living wagon. Whilst open, her engine certainly knew it had a heavy machine to drive (Moon Rocket). When the ride was sold, her hard life continued with the Dodgems.

Devizes, 1971. Working hard.
From the Barry Brown collection.

Then in 1972, she was retired for 8 years, thinking her hard life was over, only to be restored and was put back on the road again.

She was a **'Rocket'** that became a **'Prince'** and through all of this, Albert Heal was always proud of her, and what with the restoration work, he spent money on her till the very end.

The Heal family still own her today, and have changed her name back to **'The Rocket'**. Since 2005 she has been on loan to the Dingles Steam and Fair Ground Museum in Devon, where she is leading a graceful retirement along with Albert's 100 year old living wagon.

Taken at the Dingles Museum, Devon.
Picture courtesy of Mr Jim Wells.

Within the title of this book I have stated 'THE FORGOTTEN SCAMMELLS'. It is known that the Studt family of Wales had two of the 45 ton chain drives, yet I have never seen a picture before of either of these Scammells. I have managed to contact Harry Studt and Peter Studt, who have confirmed the 2 Scammell purchases. I asked the family if anyone had previously enquired with the intention to write about either Scammells, only to be told no, so I am wondering if these two really are THE FORGOTTEN SCAMMELLS.

Well not today, as here I can reveal their names and numbers and have accounted for them as being 2 of the 10 that went to the showmen.

SCAMMELL 4

'Earl Kitchener' JC 8358

Courtesy of the Harry Studt collection.

In May 1946, Showman Arthur L Studt of Pwllheli Gwynedd, North Wales, purchased chassis number 1964.

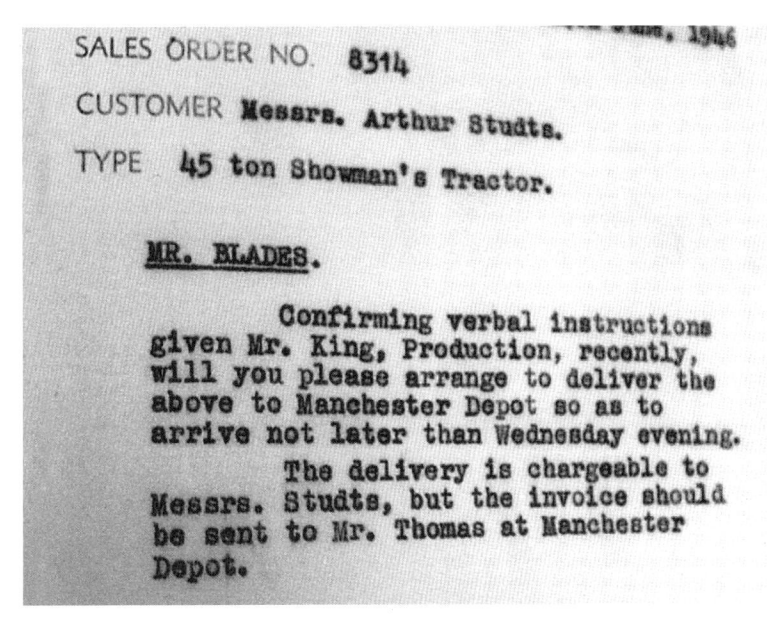

```
SALES ORDER NO.  8314
CUSTOMER  Messrs. Arthur Studts.
TYPE  45 ton Showman's Tractor.

MR. BLADES.
            Confirming verbal instructions
given Mr. King, Production, recently,
will you please arrange to deliver the
above to Manchester Depot so as to
arrive not later than Wednesday evening.
            The delivery is chargeable to
Messrs. Studts, but the invoice should
be sent to Mr. Thomas at Manchester
Depot.
```

Arthur named her Earl Kitchener, which was after a traction engine the family used to own. The name plate from the original engine was placed on her radiator.

The ballast box style body which was delivered at a later date.

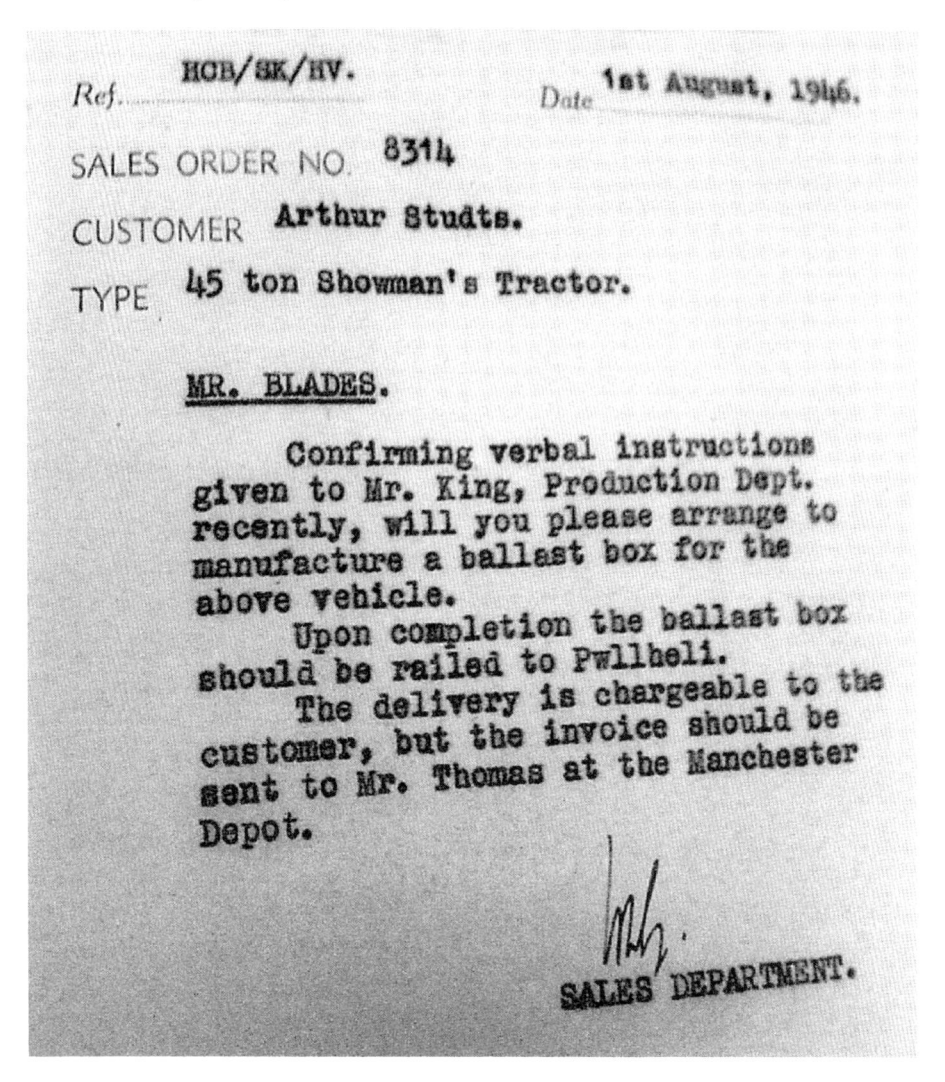

Ref. HOB/SK/HV.
Date 1st August, 1946.

SALES ORDER NO. 8314

CUSTOMER Arthur Studts.

TYPE 45 ton Showman's Tractor.

MR. BLADES.

Confirming verbal instructions given to Mr. King, Production Dept. recently, will you please arrange to manufacture a ballast box for the above vehicle.
Upon completion the ballast box should be railed to Pwllheli.
The delivery is chargeable to the customer, but the invoice should be sent to Mr. Thomas at the Manchester Depot.

SALES DEPARTMENT.

She did not come with a winch or dynamo, so the family put the dynamo from their traction engine on her instead.

Her body was maroon with gold leaf lining and monogram.

***Here she is towing her 3 Dodgem trucks from Clydach
to Ystalyfera around 1963.***
From the Harry Studt collection.

Her job was to tow and power the family Dodgems and also the Orton & Spooner Ark ride, which was eventually altered to a Waltzer. Normally she would tow 2 trucks, except on short journeys when she would take 3 trucks. As you can see in the picture above, she was on one of her shorter journeys with 3 trucks. Again I must mention the terrible brakes these lorries had. Harry Studt, who was only 27 at the time, was driving her down a winding road in North Wales, when she started to gather speed. Thankfully the brakes on the 2 trucks helped to bring her to a halt half way down the hill. Because the road was so winding, if she had not been stopped, the outcome could have been tragic...

Something happened with this one that I have never known with any of the others. Whilst open one day, Arthur climbed upon the back while her dynamo was running, he was wearing a long dust coat at the time and the coat caught in the chains as they were turning and pulled him closer into the dynamo. Thankfully Arthur was a strong man, and managed to pull himself free.

In 1964, the family decided to settle down in Pwllheli, and open June until September as a permanent Amusement Park. Because the lorries became redundant, the Scammell was eventually sold in about 1970 as scrap and her 6 L W Gardner engine was used to make up a generator for the Amusement Park.

SCAMMELL 5

'John Bull' EYC 38

Sketch by Louise Mowlem.

In 1946, Showman John Peter Studt of Swansea, purchased chassis number 1963 and named her ***'John Bull'***.

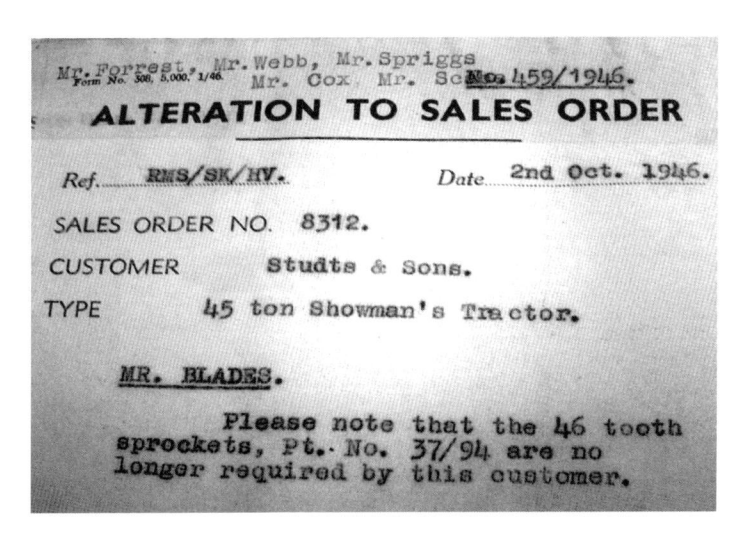

```
Mr. Forrest, Mr. Webb, Mr. Spriggs
                Mr. Cox  Mr. Sc  No. 459/1946.

ALTERATION TO SALES ORDER

Ref.  RMS/SK/HV.              Date  2nd Oct. 1946.

SALES ORDER NO.  8312.

CUSTOMER         Studts & Sons.

TYPE             45 ton Showman's Tractor.


       MR. BLADES.

              Please note that the 46 tooth
       sprockets, Pt. No. 37/94 are no
       longer required by this customer.
```

She did not come with the winch or dynamo so the dynamo off their traction engine, which was a Mather & Platt dynamo, was put on the back of her instead. A problem they did have when the dynamo was running, was the vibration of the engine, which made the hand throttle on the steering wheel move. So they drilled a hole so a pin could be put through to stop it moving.

The hand throttle.

Her colour was crimson red with gold leaf lining. The body was the ballast box style, which John Peter Studt built himself. Her job was to tow and power the family's Dodgems.

John Peter's son, Peter, drove the Scammell for a number of years, as when Peter was 17 his father passed away, so Peter had the responsibility of driving the Scammell before he was supposed to (the legal age being 21). His mother would make him wear a trilby hat when driving, to make him look older at the wheel. Peter Studt described the Scammell as terrible to drive.

Whilst writing this book and listening to the drivers, I now know how hard these Scammells were to drive and what could go wrong. Young Peter, at 17, had a big responsibility on his shoulders every time he climbed into the cab. Peter can remember well how poor the brakes were. Whilst he was driving through Pembrokeshire, there were road works and Peter had to drive on the wrong side of the road to pass them, also there was mud on the road and it was up hill. The Scammell started to slip on the mud and with the weight of the 2 Dodgem trucks she was towing, was pulling her backwards. There was nothing Peter could do. Luckily the family also had a Matador lorry, which was behind him at the time and they could see what was happening. So they quickly put blocks behind the wheels. As she was sliding very slowly, the blocks stopped her. As she was now stuck half way up the hill, they put a straight bar on the front of the Matador leading to the back truck and the Matador helped by pushing the complete load up the hill. A few days before, Peter, whilst carrying a tea chest, had fallen and cut his hand badly. He had to have stitches across his palm, therefore he could not use the Scammell hand brake, so another showman acted as pilot for the hand brake. Peter said "It was a most terrible experience on that hill."

In the 1960s, the family decided it was time for the lorry to go, the Scammell and Matador were sold to a scrap dealer in Cardiff, who wanted the Scammell for her engine.

SCAMMELL 6

'Earl Beatty' CJY 965

From the George Devey collection.

George Devey and Gilbert Smith, who was part of the West Country partnership of Anderton & Rowland, acquired the one known as Earl Beatty, chassis no 1960, on the 27th May 1946, through the agent Sidney Harrison. She was named after one of the family's previous traction engines, Burrell No. 2896, Reg CO4052.

When new, they decided not to have the winch. However, they did put a dynamo on the back of her, which was only used as a standby, so it was not used very much.

At first there was no body on her, just the dynamo and a spare wheel. A chariot body was fitted to her in 1954, by George Hearly at his workshop at Plymouth.

From the George Devey collection.

During her life, Earl Beatty travelled around Devon, Cornwall, Somerset and Dorset.

In her early years, her main job was to tow 2 heavy Dodgem trucks, and Gilbert Smith's living wagon. *'Earl Beatty'* also worked along side the Showtrac they purchased in 1947, called *'John Bull'*. Both Scammells were used with the Dodgems. Everyone's opinion is different, but I have been told by two people who drove both Scammells, that the chain drive was preferred for doing the shunting, as her nose was longer than the Showtrac, and you could follow the line of the truck better with the truck draw bar coupled to the front. Also because of the tube axle on the chain drive, it enabled a tighter lock, whereas the dropforge axle on the Showtrac did not provide such a tight lock. It was decided *'Earl Beatty's'* front coupling was too high when shunting the trucks, so they had it lowered by about 8 inches.

On a good road of course, the Showtrac was better, because of the 6 speed box and it was shaft driven. However on bad hilly roads the strength of the 45 ton chain drive was preferred.

We have already mentioned how bad the brakes were on the chain drive, and on one occasion with young George Devey and Geoff Lewis in the cab travelling from Babbacombe, to Torquay, she picked up too much speed going down a hill. Trying to stop her by feathering the foot brake as well as using the hand brake was proving a little difficult, also the road being damp and greasy at the time did not help. When they reached the bottom of the hill, the Scammell ended up turning side ways and came to a halt. Thankfully, she was not towing anything at the time, but if she had been, heaven knows what the outcome would have been.

For a few weeks each summer, she would leave the Dodgems, as George Devey senior would need her in order to use her dynamo. He would take her from Taunton to Looe in Cornwall, when the summer season was busy and he needed more power for his Ark ride.

Because the dynamo was not used very much, in later years it was decided to put two complete generators on the back instead, one of which originally came from the Olympia Showman's Exhibition and was a Harrison 4 cylinder Gardner which Sidney Harrison sold to West of England showman Jack Panell, who then sold it to Anderton & Rowlands. The other one was made by showman Jimmy Miller at Bristol and was a 5 cylinder Gardner.

Shaldon, Devon, 1964.

She could not have had the chariot body for more than 10 years, as on this page it has been removed.
From the Barry Brown collection.

From the George Devey collection.

Sherborne Pack Monday Fair 1969.
From the Alan Imber collection.

She had a new cab in the 1960s, built by the brothers, John and Rowland Anderton. She was taken to Mill Street, Crediton for the work to be done. The peak over the cab windscreen, was not replaced on the new cab.

Nr, Launceston, 1974.
From the Nigel Vanstone collection.

Notice the new cab, with no peak.

Coming to the end of her days on the road, Taunton 1975.
Courtesy of Mr Barry Brown.

After 30 years of service to the Anderton & Rowland family, she was retired and was taken to the yard at Gloucester Lane, Bristol, where she stood covered over with canvas for 27 years, along with the family's retired Showtrac the *'John Bull'*. Vandals damaged both *'Earl Beatty'* and the *'John Bull'* whilst the family were away travelling, so in 2002, both Scammells were moved.

The day of the move

World's Fair Correspondent, Mr Ernie Taylor reported the event in 2002 and he has kindly given me permission to convey extracts and photos from his article.

On a horribly wet Sunday two recovery vehicles arrived at the Gloucester Lane Yard.

The object of the exercise was to remove two Scammell tractors, which had been laid up for a number of years. The vehicles in question was chain drive CJY 965 'Earl Beatty' and Showtrac 'John Bull'. Since the yard has ceased to be in regular use the undergrowth had grown to almost jungle like proportions. Hence a workforce were on hand with a saw for deforestation.

Earl Beatty not looking very well, but seeing the light again after 27 years.

*All three photographs accompanying this extract
by kind permission of Mr Ernie Taylor.*

So much hacking and sawing took place to release them from bondage. 'Earl Beatty' proved to be difficult, but was eventually pulled out beside the 'John Bull'. But in view of the wet slippery conditions it was decided to low load 'Earl Beatty', also it being considered unwise to tow in case the chains seized while on the road.

'Earl Beatty' has not been in use by the family for many years now, and yet they have not parted with her.

At the time of this publication in 2007, this old lady has stood the test of time and survived and she is in need of restoration. But can we can look forward to the day, when we will all be able to see her again?

SCAMMELL 7

'Dreadnought' GFJ 331

By Phillip Bradley. © Surrey History Centre.

West Country showman Tommy Whitelegg bought, on 25th April 1946, 2 of the 45 ton chain drive Scammells. This one was known as *'Dreadnought'*, chassis number 1956. She did not come with the dynamo, as he wanted to put a generator on the back. She came with the winch, which was not complete. Later in time young Bibsy Whitelegg drove her from Exeter, to the Scammell works at Watford for the winch rope to be fitted. The journey seemed to take forever because she was so slow. The generator had to be raised up, so the winch rope could feed along under the generator.

Two of these chain drives were bought by Tommy Whitelegg, the other being ***'Impregnable'***.

Tommy and his wife Rose.
From the Guy Belshaw collection.

The firm of Whiteleggs was large and they owned many lorries over the years, so large that there were 2 parts to the business. ***'Dreadnought'*** would travel with the 2nd part, towing and supplying the power to the Waltzer, which was one of the first Waltzers in the country, later to be converted to an Ark. Tommy's son Bibsy, was given charge of ***'Dreadnought'***, it was his responsibility to drive and look after her whilst on the road.

Tommy's son Bibsy Whitelegg senior.
From the young Bibsy Whitelegg collection.

'Impregnable' and **'Dreadnought'** would work alongside each other for the regatta fairs. They would start the season at Central Park, Plymouth at Easter. The 2 lorries would be together for about 4 weeks, then the family went their separate ways, so to cover as many fairs as they could, meeting up only occasionally for the bigger fairs like Penzance, Helston, and Torbay regatta. Both Scammells were the same livery of crimson with red mudguards and yellow lettering.

'Dreadnought' taken between Yelverton and Rowbrough,
heading for Plymouth, 1958.
By Phillip Bradley. © Surrey History Centre.

Unfortunately there were 3 runaways with this one. On one occasion they had stopped at the top of Haldon Hill, between Exeter and Plymouth, for a cup of tea at a café. Then they set off down the hill. Young Bibsy Whitelegg was driving her at the time. He kept her speed down using bottom gear.

He told me "It took as long to down a hill as it did to go up one." They now had air brakes fitted to the trucks. When young Bibsy applied the brake, he found there was no brake, as the air brake pipe had come detached from the bottom of the truck, and had been dragging on the ground for some time creating a hole, consequently when going down the hill, the truck brake held no vacuum.

Bibsy could feel she was gaining speed. He decided to take her out of gear, doing about 25mph. I asked why he took her out of gear? He told me, "_In gear_ she is trying to hold back the trucks and is being pushed forward by them, then the back truck starts to sway, followed by the second truck and you end up with a dangerous load swaying all over the road pushing you forward. Out of gear, letting her run free, the speed of the lorry is pulling the trucks forward, so less swaying and you can keep a straighter load, but you must hope at the bottom of the hill you can somehow regain control."

Bibsy told the chap with him to open the door and jump out, but he would not abandon Bibsy with the load.

She was travelling at such speed, the chains were rattling and making so much noise, Bibsy said, "I thought they were going to come off."

At the bottom of the hill is another hill called the Wobbly Wheel. As they climbed it and started to slow, the chap in the passenger seat jumped out and threw a block with a chain attached under the wheel. As the lorry went over it, he would pull it out again quickly running along side the lorry, and would throw it back in front the wheel again, until she stopped. They had to pull over for 45 minutes before Bibsy attempted to start her again, as she was so hot, also the radiator was making terrible noises. They took it steady for the rest of the journey with there being no truck brakes. I have also been told, when she had done a long journey, the chains were so hot, that when she was turned off, you could hear the hot chains making pinging noises as they cooled, also the radiator would sing when it was hot, I have not known this on any of the others.

I met young Bibsy Whitelegg, now in his 70s, in April 2007. I got the impression that he was a strong-minded man who had been through a lot, and got on with life. Reading the above story I think my impressions were right, and he also is a lovely man to talk to.

The second runaway occurred while going down a hill at Mevagissey, in Cornwall.

This time to slow her down, Bibsy mounted the grass verge so he could run her against the hedge. Hoping the front corner of the truck being towed, would clip the hedge to help slow her down, which it did.

The third time was going down into Kingsbridge, Devon. As the roads were so narrow and winding, Bibsy used the transmission foot brake a few times, but when he came to a hill, the foot brake was already hot and not working at all. The cab was filled with smoke and fumes as Bibsy kept trying the brake. He needed to slow her down as he could see Tommy's load in front, and he was gaining on him and getting a little too close for comfort. Luckily on Tommy's truck, long sleepers which were part of the bottom of the Dodgem track floor, were packed / pushed in at the bottom of the truck, sticking out a little. Bibsy managed to slow by now but he could not completely stop her, so Bibsy gently went into the back of Tommy's truck, touching the sleepers sticking out of the truck. So going down over the hill Tommy's brakes were holding both of them. Thankfully no damage was done to anything. Tommy knew nothing about all this until Bibsy told him what had happened.

One day coming away from Salisbury, the bolt holding the fan on came loose. The fan did not go through the front of the radiator, but instead went side ways, snapping off one of the fan blades. Luckily as they were towing the Ark, they had plenty of bolts to hand, so they bolted the three bladed fan back in place, but now the engine boiled and they needed plenty of water. It happened on a hill called Wynyards Gap (which I mentioned in my last book). At the bottom of the hill, there was a stream, so they washed out some empty 5-gallon oil drums, and filled them with water.

Near the end of her life, Holesworthy, 9th July 1959.
By Phillip Bradley. © Surrey History centre

'Dreadnought' would winter at their yard in Cowick Street, Exeter, and that is where she was cut up for scrap.

The Dreadnought had a short life, bought new through the Scammell rep, Sidney Harrison, in April 1946, and then she was scrapped in the late 50s. Her working life was so short because the family were updating their transport to the faster ERF. The only thing that still exists is **'Dreadnought's'** winch, which is on Tommy Rowland's lorry.

SCAMMELL 8

'Impregnable' GFJ 330

Totnes 1953
By Phillip Bradley. © Surrey History Centre.

West Country showman, Tommy Whitelegg, on the 25th April 1946, purchased the one known as *'Impregnable'* chassis number 1957. When Sidney Harrison put the 10 Scammells up for sale, Tommy bought the first two.

'Impregnable' was named after a Naval training ship at Devonport Dockyard.

She came with the winch and 400 amp Mawdsleys dynamo. *'Impregnable'* travelled around Devon and Cornwall fairs. Her job was to work with and tow the Whitelegg's No 1 set of Dodgems. You will notice in the picture above, V belts are hanging beneath the lorry. This is because they did not use the chains on the dynamo when powering the Dodgems. Instead a larger pulley was placed on the dynamo, then V belts were used instead of chains (which was quieter running than the chains). These belts were not removed from the lorry. On the road they were disconnected from the dynamo and tied up from the road by thin rope.

Also in the photo above, she has chrome hub caps, these were mentioned as standard on the order sheets when new, but you rarely see them on the other Scammells.

From the Barry Brown collection.

This is an interesting photo. In the late 50s the dynamo was taken off and a chariot body was added. Two generators replaced the dynamo. Pictured in the front, her driver Bob Pepper.

She did little mileage compared to the others, as she only covered two counties, then was retired in 1965. Then she stood in the corner of their yard at Cowick Street, Exeter. Over the next 14 years she deteriorated badly out in the open. A Mr Mike Stabbs of Brixham, Devon, used to repair and maintain the Whitelegg lorries and wagons during the winter months at the Whittlegg's yard. Although she looked pretty bad, Mike still admired the Scammell and thought how he would like to restore her. He did mention several times about buying the old Scammell, but the reply was, "She would cost a lot of money to do and has done her days' work." So for 14 years she stood in the corner of the yard untouched as the brambles grew around her. Then in 1979 Mike Stabbs' dream finally came true and he bought her. By now the long standing had taken its toll.

From the Mike Stabb collection.

She had no engine, so an old generator with a 6 LW Gardner was taken apart so the engine could be put in the Scammell. Such as the bonnet was found in the bushes and had been trampled on. Many parts were missing, old Frank Edwards helped by supplying the thrust bearings ect. The restoration took about two and a half years. Now she is how she was originally.

From the Barry Brown collection.

Shunting her original truck which Mike has also purchased.
From the Mike Stabb collection.

Mike has been rallying her for many years now, and as you can see in the picture above, full credit has to be given to Mike and his family, for doing a wonderful job of restoring her. Of course she has those messy chains, and when Mike has taken her on a long journey such as to the Dorset Steam Fair, the first thing he has to do is to wipe her down with white spirit to remove the grease that the chains have flapped everywhere.

As Tommy Whitelegg has passed away, we do not know of any runaways with this one during the early years, in fact we don't think there were any, as she had a quiet life. However her owner now, Mike Stabbs was going down Halden Hill with his rare Macalister & Hunter living wagon, when she jumped out of gear and started to run away. Fortunately when he reached the bottom of the hill and then started to climb the next hill, she slowed enough for Mike to get her back into gear. It was still a frightening experience for Mike. At the time of writing this book, I have not seen **'Impregnable'** yet, but I look forward to the day when I will.

SCAMMELL 9

'The Mascot' DDT 32

From the New Era collection.

What they really wanted

(I would like to thank Mr. Tom Harniess for the information below)

In 1945, the Showmen were experiencing the post war boom when everyone was spending money and celebrating the end of the war. This busy time put many Showmen back on their feet. It was during this busy time, that Tom Harniess and his father Frank both agreed to contact Watford and order 4 Showtracs. Scammell contacted them to say they could not deliver all 4 in time for the start of the season (pulling out at Easter). However, they could deliver 2 chain drives and then 2 Showtracs at a later date, so Tom Harniess agreed to this.

So chain drive DDT 32, chassis No 1959, was ordered from Sidney Harrison by the late Frank Harniess of Doncaster. I say late, as he did not see delivery of DDT 32, as Frank passed away before she came.

The Harniess family in York 1943

Frank   **Young Tom**   **Tom**

Both Toms, seen in this picture, drove DDT 32
From the Tom Harniess collection.

His son Tom, who also ordered one of the models himself, decided to allow his father's purchase to go ahead, so on the 13th April 1946, Tom Harniess, collected the first of his chain drives (the one that would have belonged to his father). Her name *'Mascot'* came from a previous traction engine that the family had owned. The Scammell was bought for working with and towing the Harniess Orton & Spooner Dodgems.

I would like to clarify some confusion here. DDT 32, has always been known as the ex Frank Harniess Scammell, yet he never actually saw her (as I have explained). A cousin also called Frank, travelled with the family and some thought that it was his Scammell, but as I have said it now belonged to Frank's son Tom.

When new, she had the dynamo complete with switch board. On the order sheet from the Leyland Museum, it states she had the winch and skid chains, which were chains that fitted over the tyres to improve the grip on soft ground. There is no mention of skid chains being ordered with any of the other Scammells in this book (however this was an option when ordering the next model after this one, the Showtrac). Tom Harniess can remember well how difficult the chain drive was to drive. When on soft ground with skid chains on, she would move anywhere, if not towing anything.

When using her winch and snatch blocks, if a vehicle was bogged down to the axles, she would still pull it out with little difficulty. Today Tom refers to her as a good reliable lorry.

The Harniess family were very careful drivers and fortunately did not have any runaways or mishaps with this one.

In later years when Tom's son, young Tom Harniess, was about to drive her, his father tutored him well on the dos and don'ts, and the dangers with this lorry. He was not allowed behind the wheel until he had understood everything his father had told him.

In about 1966, Tom sold his Dodgems to Mr Gordon Eddy along with one Showtrac and Scammell DDT 32.

As soon as Gordon Eddy got into the cab and drove the chain drive for the first time, he disliked the lorry straight away, he could not believe what he had bought. I was told his words were, "My God what have I bought?" as she was terrible to drive and he only got 15mph tops.

His son Raymond Eddy told me that he could remember when changing from 1st to 2nd gear, the chains flapped. You had to take her out of 1st gear and allow her to slow until the chains stopped flapping – only then could you go into 2nd gear.

After only one year, Gordon Eddy sold her for £150 to a Mr Gerry Procter of York.

The World's Fair, Saturday 7th January 1967.

```
FOR SALE              FOR SALE

         14ft. HOOPLA
Nicely decorated. Fitted night
shutters. Together with 20 assorted
         boxes, mostly fruits.
Some positions if required, includ-
    ing 26ft. postion at Newcastle

              ALSO

          CHAIN DRIVE
     SCAMMELL TRACTOR
First reg. 1947. Fitted winch and
good 6LW Gardner engine. Would
suit traction engine enthusiast for
        transporting same.

          Apply G. EDDY
Fair Ground, Wesley Square
         Goole, Yorkshire
```

Now she did not belong to a showman any more.

Mr Procter wanted her for towing an artic trailer to take his steam roller *'Billy Boy'* to steam rallies. Mr Procter designed a complete new braking system himself from scratch, as he wanted front brakes as well. He ended up changing her front axle for one from a Thorneycroft Big Ben transporter.

From the Barry Brown collection.

In the photo you can see the Thorneycroft front axle, also air tanks he put on the back of the cab so now he had a 4 wheel braked tractor, which was compatible with his artic trailer which he intended to tow.

He rigged the artic up, by bolting the fifth wheel directly on top of the Scammell chassis, so the Scammell springs had to take the weight of the trailer as well. Before he could fit the fifth wheel, the 4 ton ballast weight bolted to the chassis, had to be removed.

In 1984, after about 17 years in his ownership, Mr Procter advertised her for sale in a steam magazine. A Mr Brian Freer saw the advert, and consequently bought the lorry complete with trailer

It came plated and tested, as Mr Procter had been using her up until he sold her.

1984, Gerry Procter (on the left) and Brian Freer, about to do the deal.
From the Ben Freer collection.

I would like to step aside from the Freer story for a moment, as there is something I would like you to know.

In 2003 Gerry Procter passed away. Towards the end he was confined to his bed, and he sat up in bed and wrote all about his Scammell, with the intention of sending the letter to the *'Old Glory'*. Gerry's son, Philip Procter and myself, would like to share Gerry's letter with you. So these are the words of Gerry Procter.

Dear Sir,

I thought some of your readers may be interested in how I come to save my old Scammell for preservation, as some interest is being shown at the moment.

After restoring 'Billy Boy', the Aveling and Porter steam roller, I decided to look around for a suitable low loader transporter. A nice interesting old vintage vehicle might be nice? Spotting an advert in the 'World's Fair' for a Scammell, I decided to have a look. I found it stood parked in a large

Continued overleaf

public car park, where the vandals had started to smash windows ect, but nothing too dramatic.

Despite looking untidy and dejected I could see some potential for a restoration job. So a deal was struck with Mr Gordon Eddy, who had introduced me to DDT 32, and I was the owner of an interesting vintage machine.

Mr Procter decided he wanted to self design a complete new braking system for the Scammell. He contacted Scammell at Watford (see letter at beginning of book, page 4) he also contacted the Ministry Test Centre for advice. His letter goes on to say:

A list of requirements was drawn up, which included the removal of the 4 ton cast iron weight, fitting a 5 ton Kirkstall axle (Delivery 18 months). Fitting a fifth wheel coupling for the trailer and designing and fitting an efficient 3 line air brake system for the whole vehicle, to give a performance in compliance with the new regulations.

After draughting a proposal, I paid a visit to the Manager of the Ministry Test Centre who proved to be a most knowledgeable and helpful gentleman. With his guidance and a few 'mods' here and there, a scheme was finalised on, that he assured me, would meet with the approval of the inspectors.

Next question, how much was all this going to cost? Quite a lot if we weren't careful and I had already given up my sweet allowance. Salvation came in the form of a local firm who were buying delivery mileage army vehicles for breaking for spares.

One vehicle provided all my needs with 'as new parts' and enabled me to do a cost effective job. Other parts I made in my own workshop and circuit diagrams and drawings only cost a bit of spare time.

While all this was going on I was looking round for a suitable swan neck trailer to complete the outfit. Eventually I found one at Elliot, Heavy Haulage, York. Even older than the tractor unit, and having seen better days, a deal was done with Mr Elliot, and it was made into quite a tidy trailer.

Soon it was time for the first test! Joining the queue with some trepidation, I noticed relatively new vehicles were failing for fairly trivial faults.

Then disaster struck! The inspector in the pit emerged to say he had found a leak that cast a shadow over the whole operation. Imagine my relief to find it was my flask of tea that had fallen over! So home we went to more adventures with DDT 32 of which there were many over the 17 years of my ownership.

Gerry passed away just a few days after writing this letter.

DDT 32 and 'Billy Boy' – their first year together.
Courtesy of Philip Procter.

Philip Procter reminisces of happy days with DDT 32

Prior to passing my HGV, I would ride in DDT 32 with my father as driver's mate. One of the highlights of going to the testing station was that the Scammell had to have her full load in ordered to be tested. So each year we would take along the low loader complete with road roller *'Billy Boy'*, as the testing stations equipment was not adequate for his self design braking system.

They always had concerns about the brakes, as the brakes were more then capable of locking the wheels. The station was always afraid of damaging their test rig!

Nevertheless, the Manager would get his staff to site along the edge of the trailer for a group photo.

From the Philip Procter collection.

1984, before she went, Gerry's last picture of her, loaded up waiting for Brian Freer to collect. A sad day for Gerry and Philip Procter after 17 years of happy rallying.

So in 1984, Brian Freer bought DDT 32 from Gerry Procter for rallying. In 1986 Brian freer found the original axle Mr Procter had taken off, it had came up for auction and Brian ended up putting the original front axle back on, so now she was back to her original set up of only having rear brakes again. However there are additional power servo air assisted brakes, which Brian has added after the removal of the auxiliary brakes Mr Procter had put on. So the tanks on the back of the cab have been removed. She still has the air hand brake. As her braking is much better then the other 45 tonners, Brian Freer has not had any mishaps when going down hills.

The rear wheels were 1400 by 20s when Brian bought her, and he has changed them to the original tyre size 40 by 8s. Brian built the ballast box body on the back himself, as Gerry Procter had removed the ballast block when he fitted his fifth wheel. So first Brian had to slot the original ballast block back between the chassis rails, before the body could be added. Notice how after 17 years, her original parts are being refitted. Brian kept the original colour of blue, and just re-lettered her in his name.

From the Ben Freer collection.

Here she is in 1986, having a little fun doing a lorry pull at the Rutland Railway Museum, Cottesmore. Towing Scammell Trunker JYM 403K, along with loco 'Dora' total about 45 ton gross. They were on their way to R.A.F. Cottesmore.

One day a man called at the yard to ask the family if he could take some pictures and measurements of the Scammell, for a project he was doing. He was given permission and returned several times to get his information correct.

Brian's neighbours went on holiday to Land's End, and on their return they said, "We think we have found your Scammell."

They took the photos (below), of her made as a land train at Land's End, taking people on sightseeing tours. Apparently he has made a good replica of her. The gentleman bought a Diahatsu FourTrac for the chassis.

Both pictures from the Ben Freer collection.

In 1987, at the Black Country Museum, Dudley, because some ex Pickford's chain driver men would be present, a lorry pull was arranged. This involved the Scammell coupled to Fowler road loco 'Atlas' towing a Scammell trailer on solid tyres, laden with crane ballast weights from a tower crane along with a dynamo and transformer. This would have totalled a weight of about 70 tons. This was then towed around the Museum grounds.

From the Ben Freer collection.

Well, if you were pulling 70 ton, wouldn't you need a little help from the engine on behind?

From the Ben Freer collection.

79

Next, she pulled a triple load, the same load as before, with ex Pickfords 45 ton chain drive, and instead of 'Atlas', with engine Lord Roberts.

I was told it brought a few tears to the eyes of the Pickford drivers, seeing such a sight.

On another occasion, at a timber rally at Petersfield, Hampshire. She towed a Crane 60 capacity ton float trailer with a Caterpillar D7 crawler aboard.

This took place on a steep grass incline, the total weight would have been around 45 tons. This time she was on small 12 teeth sprockets, so was lower geared and was able to tow more weight at a slow speed.

She pulled it OK but only just made it over the top of the hill, as she suffered wheel spin on the grass.

In 1988 she was trimmed up with bows, as she attended a family wedding, when Jim Freer was married at St. Botolph's Church, Stoke Albany, the Scammell took the groom and best man to the church.

From the Ben Freer collection.

In 1989 the family found an old 5 ton boiler on a farm. It was big so would look impressive behind the Scammell when doing the rallies. She towed the boiler on a Cranes of Dereham, solid wheel trailer.

Ben and Brian cleaning and getting the boiler ready to load.
From the Ben Freer collection.

On route for the Commercial Vehicle Rally at Rugby,
ex Pickford's GXC554 leading the way.

No longer the 'Mascot'

In 1989, the family decided to re-name her 'Sid' after a late member of the family.

81

She has travelled further then any of the others

In about 1991, the Scammell Owners and Enthusiast Club, had discussions with DAF, on the name of Scammell, of which DAF trucks had the copyright. During these discussions, DAF Management invited the Scammell owners to visit their HQ for a weekend in Eindhoven, Netherlands. About 8 lorries made the pilgrimage, travelling by ferry from Sheerness to Vlissinghen. The convoy of aged Scammells decided to unload and drive the last leg of the journey, so the convoy would enter HQ in style.

Seen here unloading for the final leg of the journey.
From the Ben Freer collection.

On arrival the management and staff treated the drivers like honoured guests; subsequently DDT 32 now carries a GB plate!

From the Barry Brown collection.

Brian rallied her regularly, up until about 1991, as a box tractor with 2 solid tyre wheel trailers behind.

The family still own her despite being made offers to part with her.

Out of the 10, this one has had a unique and exciting life and has been cherished by her last 2 owners. Remember earlier in this chapter, when Gordon Eddy did not think much of her and after only 1 year he sold her on for £150. Well, I was talking to Raymond Eddy on the phone recently regarding the old Scammell, he said "Is that old lorry still going?" my thoughts were "Still going? My God she has not stopped!"

A few words from Ben Freer

DDT 32 is showing signs of old age, as we all are! However beneath all the wrinkles, there still lurks a powerful old soldier that could still do the job it was built for over 60 years ago, but to us she is more like a family pet now.

"Yes this is my Scammell."
2007, Brian feeling proud with "Sid".
From the Ben Freer collection.

What a transformation

Out of the 10 Scammells, this one has had the biggest transformation.

SCAMMELL 10

'No.1' DDT 107

From the Peter Davis collection.

In April 1946, Showman Tom Harniess of Doncaster, son of the late Frank Harniess, collected his second chain drive DDT 107, chassis number 1949. He collected this one only 4 days after his first one (DDT 32 which we talked of in Scammell 9). Tom also paid the little extra and had the winch and 400 amp dynamo. Each new place they visited, the road chains had to be changed to the smaller dynamo chains, so her engine could be used for supplying the power at night for the Harniess's other set of Orton & Spooner Dodgems. She travelled around Yorkshire, Lincolnshire, Nottinghamshire, Derbyshire and ventured as far north as Newcastle.

From the Glen McBirnie collection.

A rare picture, both the Harniess Scammells DDT 107 and DDT 32 working together.

This picture was taken in the early years, as later a frame was built over the top of each Scammell, for packing on. As the Harniess's had 2 sets of Orton & Spooner Dodgems, DDT 107 travelled with the set being managed by Frank's sister Dora and her husband.

As most of the Harniess places of opening were farmers' fields, they were only too glad that they had the winch, as it was used many times to pull out the trucks. Also they were never without their skid chains.

This family did have a block boy, or as they called him brake boy.

I am pleased to say that there were no runaways with this one. However, she did slide on one occasion. Tom was a careful driver, while on his way to Sheffield, then he came to a steep hill into Rotherham. It had been snowing and the hill was still covered in fresh snow.

Young Frank Harniess had taken the first set of loads down over the hill OK and compacted the snow a little. However when it was Tom's turn to descend the hill with the chain drive and 2 trucks, she started to slide half way down. There was a row of houses on this hill, so he steered her towards a garden wall to slow himself down (I presume to let the tyre touch the grass verge or the wall?) but instead he went straight into a gap between two houses. Thankfully the lorry came to a stop and very little damage was done apart from a little denting on each wing.

In 1966 Tom had had the Scammell 20 years now, when he decided to sell her on. In the next 6 years after this, DDT 107 had 5 more owners, she changed hands very quickly as you will see.

In 1966 Tom Harniess sold the Scammell to someone who lived close by, a Mr Raywood of Scunthorpe, who already owned a set of Dodgems and wanted the Scammell to work with them. After only 6 months, he sold her on to Mr John Barlow of Sleaford, Lincolnshire, who also had a set of Dodgems. So DDT 107 continued to travel around the same area as Tom Harniess did. You can see from the picture below John Barlow kept the top, and re-lettered it with his name. I believe he owned her about 4 years.

Taken Donnington, Linc.
From the Barry Brown collection.

John Barlow then sold her to another showman, Mr Morley, who soon afterwards sold her to Mr G T Tuby. As Mr Morley and Mr Tuby were both attending Hull Fair, that is where she changed ownership. Mr Tuby used her dynamo straight away at Hull Fair to run some lights on his Ark while open. Then he took the Scammell home to his yard at Mexbourgh. He only bought her for the dynamo, which he intended to take off, so he stored her at Mexbourgh for a short time. In 1972, the national power strikes started. The Labour Party's annual Dinner and Dance at the Civic Hall was due a power cut on the night. The Scammell was taken to the Civic Hall and her chains were dropped for her dynamo to be used, 110 volt lights were put up in the hall, so she supplied the lights, music and microphone for the Labour Party Dance.

After the dance she was taken back to the yard and the dynamo was taken off and sent to Whitby, as a spare back-up dynamo for Mr Tuby's arcade, which was 110 volt at the time.

The Scammell was then was sold to scrap dealer Mr Bunny Smith. In 6 years, 1966 to 1972, DDT 107 had 5 owners since leaving the Harniess family. The fifth one being, in late 1972, when she was bought by Mr Jack Schofield of Retford, from the showman/scrap dealer, Bunny Smith.

At the time a Mr Dave Vickers crank shaft, had broke on his Gardner and he was going to have the engine out of the Scammell, so Jack Schofield got there just in time, as Bunny was about to cut her up to take the engine out for Mr Vickers. Jack was told he had only one week to find the money £450, which he did, so thankfully she was saved, which is just as well, as you will read later, there was more life in her yet, with the excitement yet to come.

When Jack collected her from Bunny Smith, there was no starter, so with 3 pulls on the rope and she started. But there was a problem with the radiator which leaked badly. So much so, they used 45 gallons of water to get her from Rotherham to Retford. Jack bought her at first, to tow his living wagon.

Jack still keeps the Harniess canopy / frame on her.

From the Stephen Smith Collection.

By 1984, Jack had had the Scammell 12 years, also 1984 was Jack's first year out with his Gallopers. This was also the only year he used the chain drive to tow them on the road.

Following quote from an article called *'Still galloping on - at home with Jack Schofield'*, featured in the **'Old Glory'**, November 2004.

"I was terrified of it at first and it only did 15mph. I paid someone to drive it for me, but it came in handy when I bought the Gallopers".

From the Jack Schofield collection.

During that first year towing the two Galloper trucks on the A5 ring road at Shrewsbury, Jack realised he had no driving control with the accelerator. The flange around the brake drum on the back axle had cracked.

Therefore the chains were not driving her. So Jack let her come to a stop, then applied the brakes (which due to this were not working on the nearside), then he let her slowly roll backwards, with the two trucks still behind.

He turned the wheel so she was on full lock and got to a point, all she could do is stop, consequently by doing this the two trucks were across the road .

The A5 road around Shrewsbury was blocked for two and a half hours. For two of those hours the breakdown truck was trying to reach them with some difficulty.

When they did, first they towed the load straight, so that the traffic could pass. Then, the Scammell was towed away and eventually they returned for the two trucks.

The Scammell and trucks were towed to a nearby yard. Jack and the chap with him stayed with the load, Jack sleeping in the Galloper truck. He used Galloper horse covers, as pillows, also with some pulled up his arms and legs to keep him warm, as it was a frosty night. The young chap slept in the Scammell cab, with no glass in the passenger door and the gear stick in a very personal place.

On inspection the garage found there was about 4 inches of fresh crack, the rest of the crack had been there a long time, as there was oil on it.

Crack was around rim below the chain drive cog.
From the Colin Evans collection.

The repair took 1 week and had to be cast steel welded.
From the Jack Schofield collection.

As a rule they kept to the flat roads around Derbyshire, Nottingham and Lincolnshire. In August that year 1984, heading for Chelford, Nr Macclesfield, the Scammell did a runaway.

It was the first time they had taken the Scammell across the Pennines.

When coming out of Buxton, trying to pull up one of the hills, the Scammell was struggling towing the two Galloper trucks. They needed the full power of her 100 LW Gardner engine, but the hills were so steep, that she start to die on them, so Jack had a chap sat on the front wing working the primer lever on the Gardner fuel pump. However they did completely stop for half an hour on one hill.

When they reached the top and started to go down the other side, the gear lever jumped out of mesh and she started to run away, so it was not possible to get her back into gear. When taking the corner near the Setter Dog pub, Jack said "It felt like we were doing 90mph, but I don't think it was!"

He ran the front wheel against the verge and using the handbrake as well, she gradually slowed down a little. He then started to use the transmission foot brake, which got very hot, this caused the cab to fill with smoke and fumes, so much so it looked like a fog in the cab and both men were coughing and trying to hold their head out the window, whilst descending the hill.

As it was the first year with the Gallopers, the trucks had been spray painted including the brake drums. The paint on the drums also caught fire going down the hill. Seeing flames coming out, a man stopped his camper van and told Jack his back truck was on fire, but of course it was only the paint on the drums.

Jack retired the Scammell from travelling in about 1996, and he said "I have the memories and scars to prove I have one of the 45 ton chain drives of Watford."

At the time of this publication, Jack is only using her for shunting in his yard.

This book has been interesting to write, because I was brought up with a 45 ton chain drive as a child. I know some of the showmen that had just bought the slow messy chain drives, were not happy when the Showtrac came out in the same year and was thought to be better. So why? What was all the fuss about? Let's compare the 2 models.

	SHOWTRAC	CHAIN DRIVE
Gear Box	6 speed	4 speed
Speed	27 mph (approx)	15 mph (approx)
Fuel Tank	50 gallon	30 gallon

The look of the Showtrac is more attractive to the eye, due to the compact look, yet the cab was made slightly wider, the cab being:

	SHOWTRAC	CHAIN DRIVE
Cab Width	87 inches	78 inches
Nose Length	39½ inches	55½ inches

They made the Showtrac nose shorter, by putting two of the engine cylinders behind the bulkhead (so were within the cab). They both had the same engine, except for two Showtracs. If you have the opportunity, open the door on both models, inside you will see very little difference, both being very basic inside. I know everyone's opinion is different, but two of the drivers of both models, said they preferred the chain drive for shunting, as the longer nose was better for following the line of the truck, also you could get a better tighter lock on the chain drive. I have noticed the Showtrac over the years has gained more popularity then any of the other Scammells. The Showtrac figures above are <u>slightly</u> better than the chain drive and at the time of its manufacture, it was a modern lorry for the time, but is no more. In my opinion the Showtrac is <u>over-worshipped</u> by its modern day band of followers. 18 were made as work tools for the showmen, yet only 10, 45 ton chain drives went into showland, and only 7 have survived. The chain drive worked hard for the showmen and proved its reliability and strength, yet has always had to live in the shadow of a 'God' (known as Showtrac).

Photo by Len Jefferies.　　　　　　　*Photo by Barry Brown.*

Just look at the 2 models together above.

If only they could talk

The 7 surviving chain drives have stood the test of time. Some of the drivers/owners of this model have since passed away, so this book is only some of the surviving stories, but if these lorries could talk to us, boy what they could tell us of their days with the showman. I think these grand old ladies deserve more respect, don't you?